When We Are Apart

. . . remember me,
as I do you,
with all the tenderness
which it is possible for one
to feel for another,
which no time can obliterate,
no distance alter,
but which is always the same.

— Abigail Adams

Other books by

Blue Mountain Press INC.

Come Into the Mountains, Dear Friend
by Susan Polis Schutz
I Want to Laugh, I Want to Cry
by Susan Polis Schutz
Peace Flows from the Sky
by Susan Polis Schutz
Someone Else to Love
by Susan Polis Schutz
I'm Not That Kind of Girl
by Susan Polis Schutz
Yours If You Ask
by Susan Polis Schutz
Love, Live and Share
by Susan Polis Schutz
The Language of Friendship
The Language of Love
The Language of Happiness
The Desiderata of Happiness
by Max Ehrmann
I Care About Your Happiness
by Kahlil Gibran/Mary Haskell
I Wish You Good Spaces
Gordon Lightfoot
We Are All Children Searching for Love
by Leonard Nimoy
Come Be with Me
by Leonard Nimoy
These Words Are for You
by Leonard Nimoy
Creeds to Love and Live By
On the Wings of Friendship
You've Got a Friend
Carole King
With You There and Me Here
The Dawn of Friendship
Once Only
by jonivan
Expressing Our Love
Just the Way I Am
Dolly Parton
You and Me Against the World
Paul Williams
Words of Wisdom, Words of Praise
Reach Out for Your Dreams
I Promise You My Love
Thank You for Being My Parents
A Mother's Love
A Friend Forever
gentle freedom, gentle courage
diane westlake
You Are Always My Friend
It's Nice to Know Someone Like You
by Peter McWilliams
It Isn't Always Easy
My Sister, My Friend

When We Are Apart

A collection of poems
Edited by Susan Polis Schutz

Blue Mountain Press ™

Boulder, Colorado

Library of Congress Number: 81-68586
ISBN: 0-88396-149-0

Manufactured in the United States of America
First Printing: September, 1981.
Second Printing: January, 1982.
The following works have previously appeared in Blue Mountain Arts publications:

"I haven't seen you in awhile" and "If you were here," by Susan Polis Schutz. Copyright © Continental Publications, 1974. "I sit in this chair," by Susan Polis Schutz. Copyright © Continental Publications, 1975. "Even though we live," by Susan Polis Schutz. Copyright © Continental Publications, 1978. "Though we are farther apart," by Susan Polis Schutz. Copyright © Continental Publications, 1979. "We have something special" and "Although we're apart," by Andrew Tawney. Copyright © Blue Mountain Arts, Inc., 1980. "Sometimes I get lonely," by Laine Parsons; "Although we are now apart," by E. Lori Milton; "Being friends," by Jamie Delere; "If it weren't for" and "I have a lot of wishes," by Michael Rille; "I miss you," by amanda pierce; "I want so much to see you" and "When we're not together," by Andrew Tawney. Copyright © Blue Mountain Arts, Inc., 1981. All rights reserved.

Thanks to the Blue Mountain Arts creative staff, with special thanks to Faith Hamilton.

ACKNOWLEDGMENTS are on page 62.

Blue Mountain Press INC.

P.O. Box 4549, Boulder, Colorado 80306

CONTENTS

7   Susan Polis Schutz
9   Doris Amundson Arnold
11 Laine Parsons
12 E. Lori Milton
15 Ludwig van Beethoven
16 diane westlake
17 Andrew Tawney
19 Susan Polis Schutz
20 Jamie Delere
23 Laura Lee Leyman
24 Michael Rille
25 Doris Amundson Arnold
27 Susan Polis Schutz
28 Andrew Tawney
31 Joseph R. Shaver
32 E. Lori Milton
33 Walt Whitman

35 Henry Alford
37 jonivan
39 James Hackman
40 jonivan
41 Susan Polis Schutz
43 Teresa M. Fox
44 amanda pierce
45 Rowland R. Hoskins, Jr.
47 Andrew Tawney
48 Don Anthony Olsen
49 Michael Rille
51 Susan Polis Schutz
52 Patricia Fosket
53 Joyce Brink
55 Andrew Tawney
62 Acknowledgments

Even though we live
far from each other
I always talk to you
in my thoughts
and see you
in my dreams
It doesn't matter
that we are not together
because our friendship
is such a strong part
of my life
And as long as I know that
   you are happy where you are
      I, too, am happy

— Susan Polis Schutz

It is comforting
to know that we are friends;
that we can share our thoughts
        with each other in confidence,
that we can listen and care
        for each other with love
            and concern.
It makes my heart glad
        to know that we are friends.
And I want to tell you
        how much I care and
        how often I am thinking of you.
Have a wonderful day,
        friend.

— Doris Amundson Arnold

Sometimes I get lonely
   and thinking about you helps
reminding me that there is
   a person
I cherish so very much
   always close in spirit
   even when you're
   so far away . . .

But sometimes it hurts
      even more
   to think of you . . .
   your laugh, your touch
   and to remember just
How much I miss
   your gentle face
   your tender ways
   your presence in my life

— Laine Parsons

Although we are now apart
and so far from each other, my
thoughts always return to the moments
you and I have enjoyed together.

The memories of those happy times
are as refreshing and satisfying now
as the day when they were first
experienced.

Thinking of you brings a smile to my
face and warms me even on the
coldest and loneliest of days.

It is the security from these memories
    which makes me realize . . .
the power and beauty of our
friendship.

The sharing of smiles and frowns,
tears and joy, love and laughter —
the secret success of our lives together.

So, though we may now be separated
by time and distance, I know that
our feelings span this time apart and
any difficulties that will arise.

And I look forward to that moment
when I can see the glow of your eyes,
and the smile upon your face.

— E. Lori Milton

Friends are not only together
when they are side-by-side,
even one who is far away . . .
is still in our thoughts.

— Ludwig van Beethoven

each day and night
    i feel your presence
you may not be near to touch
but you are in my mind and heart
you meet my needs so silently
i am not alone because of you

— diane westlake

We have something special
that no one
  no distance
   no time
  can take away . . .
we have each other.

— Andrew Tawney

Though we are
farther apart
from each other
than ever
we are actually
closer
to each other
than ever
Our activities
and goals
have changed
and our homes
and daily habits
have changed
but we still
have the same
souls —
in need of
one another —
in need of
our precious
friendship

— Susan Polis Schutz

JUST A THOUGHT AWAY

Being friends
comes so naturally to us —
We're always there for each other,
and it's never a chore, it's done
                    from desire;
never an effort, but always a pleasure.
We've been friends
for quite awhile now,
and I'm sure that you know what I mean
when I say that
    the memories that we've got
are some of the finest I ever
                    hope to have.

It makes me glad to think
that you'll be with me
    and I'll be with you
        as friends . . .

to face the new times ahead,
   to share the wonders they will bring,
      to confront whatever trials they may hold.

It's nice to know
     you'll always have me
     caring for you,
and I'll always have you
     just a thought away.

— Jamie Delere

My friend,
we have come such a long way
in the time that we've
   known each other.
We've given each other encouragement
and have accomplished things
that we never thought we could do.
I have become a better person
   since knowing you.
You have given me many things
which I will treasure for a lifetime,
and the most important thing of all
   is the gift of your friendship.

— Laura Lee Leyman

If it weren't for
special friends like you . . .

the world would have
   no rainbows.
Thanks for lighting up my life.

— Michael Rille

I just wanted to send this
because today
I thought about you
and about what our friendship
means to me.
About how we give
   each other encouragement.
We can sense a longing.
We listen
to each other's inner thoughts
   with love and concern,
   and without giving any judgment.
We try to comfort
each other's hurts.
But best of all,
we can find companionship,
even in silence.

Our friendship
         means a lot to me.

                    — Doris Amundson Arnold

I haven't seen you in awhile
yet I often imagine
all your expressions

I haven't spoken to you recently
but many times
I hear your thoughts

Good friends must not always
            be together
It is the feeling of oneness
            when distant
that proves a lasting friendship

— Susan Polis Schutz

I want so much to see you . . .
  if only for awhile

to tell you face to face
how much I miss
my special friend
whose life is such a part of mine

I want so much to see you . . .
   if only for awhile
to reminisce about our days gone by,
and catch up on all the news
I've yet to hear

I want so much to see you . . .
   if only for awhile
and talk as we used to . . .
of our lives
our loves
our cares and concerns . . .

I want so much to see you . . .
   if only for awhile
to share some coffee in the morningside
   some memories of our togetherness
   some wishes that have since come true
   and some worries that never occurred

I want so much to see you . . .
   if only for awhile
to remind you that
no matter how far
distance separates us,
the nearness of your spirit
is always with me

I want so much to see you . . .
   if only for awhile
to feel the joy
you always bring
and the love found in your smile

— Andrew Tawney

Far away friends
    are good to have.
They sometimes surprise your mornings
with gifts or cards
    or just a call . . .
their voices and words
from miles away
want to bring a sparkle to your eyes
and a smile to your face,
reminding you
    how often you are thought of.

— Joseph R. Shaver

The distance between us
only makes me realize
more each day
how very important
you are
    to my life.

I can't put into words
all the special feelings I hold for you
    in my heart.
But until I see you again,
    please remember that
my memories and dreams
are forever filled
    with the beautiful thought
        of you.

— E. Lori Milton

I keep thinking
about you
every few minutes
all day.

— Walt Whitman

You and I

We ought to be together, you and I;

We want each other so, to comprehend
   The dream, the hope, things planned,
      or seen, or wrought.

Companion, comforter and guide
      and friend,
   As much as love asks love, does
      thought ask thought.

Life is so short, so fast the lone
      hours fly,

We ought to be together, you and I.

— Henry Alford

Wanting to see you again
makes me think of how much
we have grown
and how far we have come . . .
remaining with each other
    in mind.
Though your times and mine
have changed,
I know that we will
never lose touch with each other.

— jonivan

Every day I live
I discover
more and more
how impossible it is
for me
to live without you.

— James Hackman

I wish I could stop dreams,
Pull them out,
Shape them in front of me.
If this feat I could accomplish,
You would be here,
Instead of there.

— jonivan

If you were here
I would say thank you
Thank you for
knowing me

If you were here
I would say thank you
Thank you for
understanding me

If you were here
I would say thank you
Thank you for
making me so happy

But since you are away
I'll just think of you softly
and thank you
in my dreams

— Susan Polis Schutz

You're that special kind of friend
that everyone wishes they could have.
I always know when we're apart
    that we're still so close,
and when we're together
our time will be spent
        enjoying it to the fullest.

It's not everyone that can
        have a special friend
            like you.
I'm proud to say
        that I do.

— Teresa M. Fox

I miss you
more than words can say.
Yet, it is comforting
to know that the memories
of the times we've shared
can never be replaced.
And it reassures me to know
that the heartfelt union
we have between us
will carry me through
these lonely times
I seem to spend
thinking . . . of you.

— amanda pierce

Today . . . I have thought about you so much.
I have missed you and cherished you.
I have dreamed countless dreams of
    you and I together,
reaching for clouds and searching for stars
so that we may see and climb even higher.
I have encountered a hundred little things
that I wanted to share with you,
but you were not there,
and it made me appreciate you
and our times together even more.
Yet still, I will save all of these things
in my mind and in my heart, so that I may
share all that I am with you
in the opportunities I receive.

— Rowland R. Hoskins, Jr.

Although we're apart,
I'm never really apart from you . . .
even though distance separates us
and time finds us on our
individual paths.

Every day I sense that
we are together,
in daylight or in dream,
for kindred souls like ours
can never truly separate.

Being apart from you
is something I cannot be . . .
    for you
    are a part of me.

— Andrew Tawney

If I could touch you
across the distance
I surely would . . .
My arms reach out to hold you
across the miles;
my feelings reach out
to soothe you when you're lonely;
my soul reaches out to you,
to be your companion
who will be with you always.

Don Anthony Olsen

I have a lot of wishes
   when it comes to you
Some of them will never be granted,
         I'm sure,
but I'll go on wishing them anyway
Wishing for . . .
   life to be easy for you,
   because you make it
   so easy for everyone else

   wishing for happiness to find you,
   because you give so much to others

   wishing for smiles to be at your side,
   and rainbows to be on your horizons . . .

And of all the wishes
I'd like to come true, I wish you knew
of the love
   I'd like to send to you

                    — Michael Rille

I sit
in this chair
in my house
in this city
far away
from you
I vividly
picture you
sitting
in that chair
in your house
in your city
And though
I miss you
desperately
we are
together
in my thoughts

— Susan Polis Schutz

I wonder
if you, too
have quiet moments,
times when old memories
        find you
I wonder if you
        think of me . . .

I hope you do,
for the good times
        that we shared
            were truly good . . .
and I will never forget you.

— Patricia Fosket

So often I sit and think
about the way things were —
The fun and friends,
the joy we all had
    and the times of just being together . . .
Of course there were some days,
times we wondered how we made it.
But our friendship helped us through.

Now we may be separated,
but the bond is still there.
Friendship holds us
        together.

— Joyce Brink

When we're not together . . .
my thoughts drift alongside
    memories of you;
    things we've done and
    the way you smile so brightly
helps me forget my worries
and celebrates our wonders

When we're not together . . .
my moods come into play
    more often
and make me yearn
    for the strength
I feel with you . . .
the security I find in your eyes

When we're not together . . .
I sometimes feel so very alone,
for myself and for you . . .
imagining you being without
my loving feelings,
as I am without yours

(continued)

When we're not together . . .
my best wishes
    still go with you always

I wish to share in
    your excitements
and want to comfort your hurts
and need to be reassured that
you're keeping warm and well

When we're not together . . .
I always wonder how you are;
what you're doing and
whether you're as happy
as my heart hopes you might be

When we're not together . . .
I hold you close in
    my imagination
and remember you —
    so very often

I'll always remember
    the many moments
we've shared
and the many reasons
I care about you

(continued)

When we're not together . . .
I find myself thinking of you
at different times —
when I look through
   the day's mail,
when the phone rings
   on a lonely night
whenever any little thing
   reminds me of us

I hope you still know
how my love goes with you
from the most special
place in my heart
to wherever you may go

(continued)

When we're not together. . .
through the daily journey,
we will still look forward
to the moments
when our paths
   come together again

You must never forget
how constantly you are in
   my thoughts

For when we're not together . . .
I seem to spend my time
wishing that we were.

— Andrew Tawney

ACKNOWLEDGMENTS

We gratefully acknowledge the permission granted by the following authors, publishers and authors' representatives to reprint poems and excerpts from their publications.

Doris Amundson Arnold for "It is comforting to know" and for "I just wanted to send this," by Doris Amundson Arnold. Copyright © Doris Amundson Arnold, 1981. All rights reserved. Reprinted by permission.

diane westlake for "each day and night," by diane westlake. Copyright © Diane Westlake, 1977. All rights reserved. Reprinted by permission.

Laura Lee Leyman for "My friend," by Laura Lee Leyman. Copyright © Laura Lee Leyman, 1981. All rights reserved. Reprinted by permission.

Joseph R. Shaver for "Far away friends," by Joseph R. Shaver. Copyright © Joseph R. Shaver, 1981. All rights reserved. Reprinted by permission.

E. Lori Milton for "The distance between us," by E. Lori Milton. Copyright © E. Lori Milton, 1981. All rights reserved. Reprinted by permission.

jonivan for "Wanting to see you again," by jonivan. Copyright © jonivan, 1981. And for "I wish I could stop dreams," by jonivan. Copyright © jonivan, 1978. All rights reserved. Reprinted by permission.

Teresa M. Fox for "You're that special kind of friend," by Teresa M. Fox. Copyright © Teresa M. Fox, 1981. All rights reserved. Reprinted by permission.

Rowland R. Hoskins, Jr. for "Today . . . I have thought," by Rowland R. Hoskins, Jr. Copyright © Rowland R. Hoskins, Jr., 1981. All rights reserved. Reprinted by permission.

Don Anthony Olsen for "If I could touch you," by Don Anthony Olsen. Copyright © Don Anthony Olsen 1981. All rights reserved. Reprinted by permission.

Patricia Fosket for "I wonder," by Patricia Fosket. Copyright © Patricia Fosket, 1981. All rights reserved. Reprinted by permission.

Joyce Brink for "So often I sit and think" by Joyce Brink. Copyright © Joyce Brink, 1981. All rights reserved. Reprinted by permission.

A careful effort has been made to trace the ownership of poems used in this anthology in order to obtain permission to reprint copyrighted material and to give proper credit to the copyright owners.

If any error or omission has occurred, it is completely inadvertent, and we would like to make corrections in future editions provided that written notification is made to the publisher: BLUE MOUNTAIN PRESS, INC., P. O. Box 4549, Boulder, Colorado 80306.